My Bondage & My Freedom

"From The Mental Institution To The Pulpit"

Table Of Contents

Dedication   4

Foreword   8

Introduction   21

Chapter One: Middle School   25

- My First Nickname
- My First Exposure To Pornography

Chapter Two: High School   39
- My Purpose
- My Calling
- My Struggle

Chapter Three: College   58
- Witchcraft
- My First Diagnosis

Chapter Four: Mental Illness   69
- Paranoia Schizophrenic

Chapter Five: My Freedom   89
- Self-Evaluation & Repentance
- Old-School Revival

Dedication

I want to dedicate this book to my mother and father, Cherice Robinson-Thurston and the Late, Alfred Lee Thurston. They are both worthy of honor and appreciation.

My mother is truly worthy of this recognition for her unconditional love towards me. I could never repay her!

She remained faithful to me throughout my journey of struggle, failure, addiction, and insanity. Although it hurt her to see me go through the things that she did, she continued to fast and pray on my behalf.

My father used to call me Lil Elroy from the Jetson's tv show as a child. As I grew into a man, I faced traumatic trials, yet he still loved and prayed for me.

My mother tolerated and endured all of the mental and emotional stress that I caused her and am forever grateful for her strength and faith in God. She stood in the gap for me against the spirit of darkness that wanted to sift me as wheat.

I dedicate this book to my mother because when others left me, she stayed right by my side. She was a constant motivation and inspiration to my soul.

I dedicate this book to my father for his endurance and discipline during some of the toughest times of my life. I honor him for the years that he pushed me to become a better man.

My mother always spoke life over me when all I could smell and see was death. She would call me a holy man of God even when I was far from God and lost in my own sensual and selfish desires.

My mother added substance to me with her unfailing love and unbending faith. She is the reason why I know what a virtuous woman and wife are.

She added years to my life because without her, I'd be permanently institutionalized, permanently immobilized, or dead. I would have never made it this far in my life without her love and kindness.

My dad always told me that I had massive potential. He told me that I should always prepare myself for when God opens the door so that I will be ready to walk through it.

Dear Dad, I am ready for what God has prepared before me, yet I am still preparing; those trials, heartaches, and moments of weakness prepared me for the doors I'd have to walk through. The door you always spoke of is opening, and within that door is a hallway filled with many other doors.

I remember you hugging me from behind and telling me that you loved me and was proud of me. It felt awkward because you didn't do it often, but I knew it was genuine.

Thank you for challenging me to be the best man that I could be, and to never settle for less. I will walk through each one of these doors until I reach the door of heaven and see you again.

I am your son, I am "the streamline," I will continue to honor the name that you've given me; I will always honor you. I am your legacy on the earth; I love you.

Dear Mom, I appreciate you more than I can ever express. Your perseverance, unfailing love, patience, and constructive, yet hard criticism saved my life.

You are a pearl, a rare gem, and a precious jewel in my sight. You are the gift that God gave me in the good and hard times; I love you.

Your Son,

The Epitome Of Your Prayers......

-Antoine D. Thurston

Foreword

The treasure you hold in your hands is the work of a man who has been beyond the brink of mental and emotional anguish and gained the victory. Similar to King David, Antoine has battled one of the most formidable giants of our time: mental illness. Schizophrenia, depression, and anxiety are the modern-day giants, rising, taunting us, and attempting to steal, kill, and destroy our purpose and God-given destiny. To defeat any giant, one must get close enough to it, face to face, and on the frontlines of the battle. Located in the northern hemisphere of the globe, lives a mighty warrior, his name is Antoine Thurston.

Antoine is a minister, motivational speaker, wealth builder, mentor, and he is also a world-changing entrepreneur. And although the demand on his life to leadership is undeniable, the frontlines of war is never easy. Even so, this book is the sword that cuts off the head of the giant and sets the captive free. Throughout many toils and snares, Antoine was unaware of the calling on his young life. His story of bravery and triumph began with the formidable weapons of witchcraft, trauma, and mental illness.

He endured multiple stages of trauma throughout his years in school and college. Psychological oppression is a wicked assault for any child to bear; nevertheless, God had a plan, and He promises never to allow us to suffer what we cannot tolerate but will provide a way of escape (*1 Corinthians 10:13*). The call of God often tries us in the fire, and it is in the Refiner's fire of trials that Antoine began to feel betrayed, unloved, and angry. But in the words of *Job 23:10*, "He knows the way that I take; when He hath tried me, I shall come forth as gold." Thus, when we discuss Antoine's mental and emotional anguish from a Scriptural context, God has a plan to free from bondage, first the man, and then, the nation.

Such is His way. When God wants to use a man for His glory, his methods may appear ruthless. Since the days of the first man, Adam, God's plan of redemptions remains paved in pain and heartache. Still, His words faithfully proclaim: "Many are the afflictions of the righteous, but the Lord will deliver him out of all of them" (*Psalm 34:19-21*).

Antoine's youth did not spare him from the war in the form of torment, adversity, and mental illness. As a matter of fact, historical Scripture notes how the call of God will often begin in childhood, and much like the ancient prophets discovered, mental illness has a sure source. Ephesians 6:12 informs us of the real battle God calls us to the frontlines to fight: "For we do not wrestle against flesh and blood, but against principalities, against powers, against the rulers of the darkness of this age, against spiritual hosts of wickedness in the heavenly places." The fallen condition of man and the sin that so easily affects us is the source of every disease, sorrow, and grief. Antoine has seen firsthand how demonic forces use the fallen condition of anger to further a destructive agenda.

Nevertheless, God has a purpose and plan for each one of us! *Jeremiah 1:5* declares the word of the LORD: "Before I formed you in the womb I knew you, before you were born I set you apart; I appointed you as a prophet to the nations." The prophet goes further to inform us of how God's plan triumphs over the fallen nature of man to conquer the snares and traps of sin. "For I know the plans I have for you," declares the Lord, "plans to prosper you and not to harm you, plans to give you hope and a future. Then you will call on me and come and pray to me, and I will listen to you.

You will seek me and find me when you seek me with all your heart" (*Jeremiah 29:11-13*). In this book, Antoine offers us the healing balm to take us from bondage to a renewed freedom where we will discover hope and a joyous future in the word of God. Scripture is clear on how sin, through Adam's disobedience, caused the fall, and the fateful inheritance of thorns and thistles in the form of physical, spiritual, and mental disease; no one escapes from the condition. In various forms, the sin nature affects everyone and every part of life. *Jeremiah 17:9* warns us of the insidious nature of sin.

"The heart is deceitful above all things, and desperately sick; who can understand it?" Therefore, it's a tireless task to seek to understand and to comprehend the depravity of the human heart soberly; we need a Savior. In order to conquer the giant of mental illness, Antoine had to wrestle with it, not only as a psychological malady, but also as a spiritual reality of another realm, a dimension the clinical world has yet to address, a supernatural empire of soul and spirit where demonic forces go undetected, leaving them free to wreak havoc under the guise of medical diagnoses. And what we don't call out by name will remain stealthy under the radar, hiding below the surface of dysfunction and inner pain. According to research, mental health disorders affect the way a person responds to the stress and demands of life.

When we lack the skills to cope with these stressors and demands, we cannot regulate own our behavior, thinking, or emotions. But is it really as simple as the act of self-regulation and self-control? The very topic of mental health is a challenging one to discuss because of the many debates and views on cause, treatment, and interventions. Millions are affected by mental illnesses every year, and of the over 46 million people in the United States plagued by mental disease, it remains a daunting discussion.
Billions of dollars are lost per year in earnings, and moreover, according to the National Alliance on

Mental Illness (NAMI), the statistics are distressing in reported cases of deaths by suicide.

Antoine has experienced the madness of trying to make meaning out of the insanity of what science tries and often fails to fully comprehend and treat. Why do mental health issues seem to be getting worse? We have evolved from the inhumane shock therapies to much newer treatments, psychotropic medications and hypnotic methodologies, but are these approaches flailing at the branches, just treating the symptoms while sidestepping the origin? Neuroscience is evidence that the brain rewires, eventually renewing itself as described in Scripture in *Romans 12:12*: "Do not conform to the pattern of this world but be transformed by the renewing of your mind. Then you will be able to test and approve what God's will is; His good, pleasing and perfect will."

In today's reactive culture, the approaches to mental health appear to do just that, treating symptoms but not fully responsive to the underlying issue of family dynamics such as child abuse, neglect, rejection, and the unresolved grief that ensues. The unfinished business of childhood leaves many individuals arrested in development and frozen at the age of the early wounding. Antoine's emotional and mental battles began early in life, and his symptoms only grew worse over time. When we look at mental illness from a holistic and spiritual perspective, it enables practitioners, Pastors, ministers, and counselors to acquire a deeper understanding of what makes a person vulnerable to mental illness. It is very often noted that awareness is curative.

Like an undetected hole in the bottom of a boat, until the source of the leak is located, all the effort in the world will not stop the ship from eventually flooding and sinking; likewise, emotional dysregulation is similar to that leaky boat. Several 'leaks' caused Antoine to flood and sink under the weight of all he would survive. Dangerous signs of his flooding soul took on demonic oppression, sorcery, cutting, and ripping the pages out the bible, demanding answers from God. The Holy Spirit is the leak detector, going to the source of the dysfunction, enlightening us with the "inside information" to better see and understand our emotions and how they directly affect our mental health and wellness. Antoine dealt with a demonic structural order that would have rendered him to be hopeless, but he is no ordinary man.

After battling a history of negative thinking, horrible encounters with the law enforcement, including being tasered by police, baker acted, thrown into mental institutions, misdiagnosed, and was given psychotropic medications. The demonic oppression grew worst, and like so many others, the side effects of all the medication were unbearable. Antoine shared with me how the black outs, weight gain, irritability, insomnia, and hearing demons left him in catatonic state, paralyzing him before enslaving him to more additional torment and shame. The battle seemed insurmountable for Antoine. Suicide seemed the only way out; that's what the voices told him, oftentimes, the devil knows your identity more than you; the enemy knew the soldier that was emerging from the fire.

The problem was not simply mental and emotional; a deeper transformation was happening, a mind renewing transformation that only fasting and prayer could accomplish. Antoine's memoir offers us a glimpse into the deceptive world of mental illness where deception and the rebellious sin of witchcraft are exposed. The calling on his life is to shine the light on the enemy's schemes. Transformation makes us unrecognizable as we press towards equilibrium, although our faith may waver, God is faithful, and His love for us is unwavering, especially in what Antoine calls the "cave moments" of life. My Bondage and My Freedom provides us with new skills to cast all our cares on Christ and to rejoice when we face various trials.

There are no quick fixes, Antoine asserts, we must grow into maturity and remain steadfast in the faith in order to transform into the image of Christ. Antoine discovered the leak. Through his harrowing journey of Baker Acts, institutions, medications, and profound confusion and dysregulation he found the source of it all; the answer is within the pages of this book. As you take this journey from bondage to freedom, the Holy Spirit will sharpen you with newfound wisdom and knowledge that will commission you with authority to fulfil the Isaiah Decree: "The Spirit of the Sovereign Lord is on me, because the Lord has anointed me to proclaim good news to the poor. He has sent me to bind up the brokenhearted, to proclaim freedom for the captives and release from darkness for the prisoners" (*Isaiah 61:1*).

Implied in this powerful memoir, with its suggestion that the current secularized approaches to combat mental illness is making strides, yet misses the mark in its understanding of the heart of the human condition, is the idea that every human being is in fact, triune: body, mind, and spirit—made in the image of God. And when the soul and spirit of the body are forsaken, so too will be the source of the leak. How can those who suffer from mental illness understand the source of their suffering if it is overlooked? And how can true healing happen when the healer is rejected and ignored? The answers to these questions require a deeper look.

Antoine invites the reader to look into the unholy alliance between treatment and cure, and the agenda that seeks profit over client health and the posterity of all those who will follow along the same stream of misdiagnoses and medical sorcery. One of the many ways Antoine succeeds is in his ability to communicate his personal story, his faith, and the realities of the darkness of mental illness. This journey from bondage to freedom presents kingdom keys and fundamental skills that will allow the reader not only to manage and regulate emotions but also the opportunity to take a spiritual pilgrimage towards the transcendent knowledge of Jehovah Rapha: the God who heals. One of the most important aspects of treatment is recognizing that God does work through therapy. The integration of theology and science is found in every aspect of life.

The valuable contributions of science in psychology reveal the awesome power and wonder of the God who works in mysterious yet obvious ways to help us improve our emotional and mental stability while enhancing our relationships to achieve balance in every area of life. Faith does not deny the presence of disease, on the contrary; James 2:14-26 declares, "faith without works is dead." Even the demonic forces believe—and tremble! Faith worked together with Antoine's choice to fight for his mental health and wellness, and it is his dedication to the process of working through his challenges that justifies and proves his faith in God. Undoubtedly then, it is our fallen nature that creates the caustic chemical imbalances.

Our mental health and physical health are one. The brain orders our biological functioning, either positively or negatively, depending upon various factors. The mind-body connection is influenced by our environment, upbringing, culture, and lifestyle. The way we think has a powerful effect on our mental health. *Proverbs 4:23* warns us to "carefully guard your thoughts because they are the source of life."

A mere thought can possibly create depression and anxiety, leading to mania, distorting one's perception. And though mental health systems are important, especially in times of crisis, how often do you think clients are told to "demolish every argument and every pretension that sets itself up against the knowledge of God...take captive every thought to make it obedient to Christ" (*2 Corinthians 10:5*)? Antoine can attest, in going from baker act institutions to the pulpit, the power to take every evil thought captive was never administered among the mind-altering psychotropic medications with its toxic side effects. The powerful life-changing and mind-renewing message of the Gospel of Jesus Christ is the real source of healing and freedom, with the only side effect being a peace that surpasses all understanding. Antoine's brokenness and psychological warfare culminated at the foot of the Cross of Christ.

We all experience the effects of living in a broken world. We are indeed blessed to glean from his very remarkable testimony that offers us the absolute truth about a world marred by sin: we all have a form of mental illness. Still, God so loved the world, that He offers us the solution. Christ came to carry our sin and shame upon Himself. He overcame sin, defeating every source of disease, ultimately sealing the leaks.

My Bondage & My Freedom; From The Mental Institution to the Pulpit is a book of hope. There is hope beyond the traps of witchcraft, pornography, depression, low self-esteem, and the spirit of suicide. The author not only lives to tell the story, but he also thrives in every aspect of life today. The purpose of the church and the body of Christ is to be salt and light. *Mathew 5:14* says, "You are the light of the world-like a city on a hilltop that cannot be hidden."

There is an unquenchable fire burning inside all of the pages of this book; it is the same fire that the Creator lit inside the author while he was yet being tried in it and through it. Victory waits beyond the shadows of trauma and disease. The victory is in Emmanuel, the Christ! It is He who sets the captives free through the intentional acts of "love, joy, peace, patience, kindness, goodness, faithfulness, gentleness, and self-control"

(*Galatians 5:22-23*). And He who the Son sets free is free indeed (*John 8:36*).

~Sandra Maria Anderson

- Author of Lessons from the Thorns: His Grace is Sufficient
- Doctor of Education in Community Care and Counseling (2021)
- Prepare and Enrich Marriage and Premarital Counseling Facilitator Certificate (2018)
- Master's degree in organizational leadership (2012)
- Bachelor's in human services (2011)
- Associates in Health Care Administration (2009)
- CEO of Love Gardens Ministries International, Inc
- Stiletto Award Recipient: Adiva Cares Foundation (9/28/2019)
- School Board of Broward County Paraprofessional Highly Qualified Certification (1992- Present)
- Keystone Award, Awarded by Professor Dr. Linda Ellington of Palm Beach Atlantic University (2012-2013)

Introduction

I am very weary of the decadence of this world. It is completely heartbreaking to witness firsthand how much hope is crumbling, morals are deteriorating, and people all over this world are committing suicide.

There is not enough empowerment, motivation, and inspiration being shared to help those who are in a dark place to break free into the light. Millions of people are desperately seeking to see the light at the end of the tunnel, and this book was written to help these individuals find it.

This book will help believers and unbelievers understand that Jeremiah 29:11 is in fruition. God has a plan for their lives despite the bondage that they are in. I also want readers to see the frailty of our morals so that we may run to God for salvation.

Each reader will learn that sin is atrocious; it's debilitating, it's a spiritual anesthetic, and it incapacitates us mentally, visually, emotionally, and physically. This book will also assist those who will receive, to understand that sometimes, our reality is just a distorted mental perception, like a broken mirror; the image is distorted.

Some people live their life looking into a broken mirror and are building it off of that perception. This book will help these individuals escape this way of life and adapt to one that is more positive and realistic.

This book will also assist readers with the power of self-evaluation and acknowledgment of one's current condition. Denial keeps a person in bondage; however, if a person decides to face the errors and bad decisions that they have made, take full responsibility for their actions, God will move on their behalf.

Despite our moral failures, God is merciful. He's a redemptive God that can and will restore the years that we have lost.

God loves us, and he is still in control, even when our lives are out of control. God has a purpose for our lives!

Through my experiences and victories, each reader will gain a new sense of hope for God and their own lives. I have survived many things in my life because of my ability to face it and embrace God's love and purpose for my life.

This book is about my life; it encourages me to go forward, and I believe that it will do the same for those who are led to read it. It is filled with my personal testimonies of how life almost devoured me, and how God stepped in and covered me.

Freedom lives in this book. It is the very epitome of how someone can lose all hope and be led astray, but then find out how much God loves them and be redeemed.

John 10:10 (NIV)

"The thief comes only to steal and kill and destroy; I have come that they may have life and have it to the full."

Chapter One
"Middle School"

I was born in Tacoma, WA, to the late Alfred Lee Thurston and Cherice Thurston. I was a handsome baby boy, yet I was also three months premature. Because of this, I was born with the need for lots of physical care and nurturing to ensure that I would develop properly and become healthier. We resided in the state of Washington because my father was in the military, but eventually, we moved back to the beautiful city of Pompano Beach, Florida. After I was born, months later, my father transitioned out of the army for personal reasons.

Fortunately, I was raised in a two-parent home. I had one sibling, my sister, Chanel. We were not spoiled but were not amongst the less fortunate either. My father had a business degree, he was also employed by a company called Media One, and my mother worked for an electric company, and she was also a very successful seamstress. They both made a very decent income together, so we lived a very nice, modest life.

Footnote: It doesn't matter how you were raised; you are not exempt from the attacks of the enemy!

During my elementary school years, I was a very skinny, well behaved little boy. I enjoyed watching Rugrats, Hey Arnold, and Doug. They always had the greatest imaginations and stories for kids my age. They were fascinating to watch. Tacos were my favorite food as a child; I loved the taste and the craft of it for some reason.

Surprisingly, I really loved the color black; It was my favorite color. To me, it has an elegant presence and feel to it. Most children my age loved vibrant colors such as blue, green, red, etc., but I was completely in awe of the color black. My favorite artist growing up was Michael Jackson. I loved his voice, his moves, and his confidence as an entertainment.

During elementary, I played little league football. My first football team was the "Pompano Beach Chiefs." I wasn't into sports that much at all, but I still played as an extra curriculum activity amongst other youth.

Footnote: I was a normal kid doing normal activities just like most children. I never prepared for demonic warfare. Parents please cover your children in prayer as much as you can, even when all appears to be well.

I actually played because of my parents. I received a few awards like "Superbowl Runner Up" and "Academic Award" and other trophies with the team.

My favorite coach for the Pompano Chiefs was Coach Nate. He always showed compassion for me and saw great potential, and he was very down to earth. During my first year of playing, I remember our team going to the South Florida Youth Football League Superbowl, but we lost the game. I wasn't affected as much by the loss in ways that many of my other teammates. However, just about all of us cried that night after losing in overtime by a few measly points.

My parents were great, but as a child, I was very curious, and eventually, one day, my curiosity opened a door that I had no idea would be so hard to close. During my second or third grade school year, I remember my father had a stash of VHS tapes. I wanted to watch something, so I put one of the tapes in.

Footnote: Keep your private "adult" materials stored away. There are no limits to what the enemy will do to a child once they are exposed to something that they do not have the power to fight against.

This was my first exposure to pornography and nudity. This was the birthing place for so many battles that I would later fight in my life.

I started middle school around the age of 12 years old. I would say that I was excited to transition into middle school, but I was definitely curious as to how different it would be from elementary school. I was open to adapting to the changes that I would face as a pre-teen, the variety of classes that I would have to grow and learn from, and meeting and engaging with new students that I have never met in my life. Some of the students would be joining me in my new middle school, but I was still aware that middle school could cause us all to change drastically with or without our consent. I was curious and ready at the same time.

I was never a troublesome child during middle school. I was a pretty good student, well-mannered, respectful, and extremely modest. I was indeed a reflection of my parents.

Footnote: School is not always the place where children battle; sometimes it's behind closed doors.

However, I did have quite a bit of a personality. I was a bit goofy, so the only trouble that I would get in was for laughing too much during lessons and disturbing my teacher and classmates.

I would disturb the entire study with my laughter and end up with a written warning. Although I had a sense of humor, I never intentionally interrupted my teacher and class. I wasn't the kid who bullied others or started fights, but I did get into at least one fight per year that I was in middle school. I never started most of these fights, yet I was defending myself in the time that I needed to. I have never rejoiced because of these particular fights, but middle school was not the place to be scared to stand up for yourself.

I did what every other kid did; crack on each other, fight, make friends, and get into mischief. I did the best that I can to adapt to my new surroundings as a 6th grader, but by the time I transitioned to the 7th grade, I had become familiar with the campus, teachers, and students.

Footnote: Sports had my attention, but it was not really my main interest. Children who are involved in sports could still be involved in private sin.

I blended right in! I was still an average kid with average expectations from school. However, I knew more students, and I knew my way around much better.

I was still very active in sports during middle school. I continued to play football for the Pompano Chiefs while in middle school in the sixth grade, and I also did track and field with the "Pompano Express" during my 6th and 7th grade year. While doing track and field, I did the shot put, disc, and the fast walk. I did relatively well with the shot put but could've been a lot better if I followed the training prescribed by coaches. I became very good friends with a kid name Dahrnaz during these times as well.

He did shot put and disc with me. Again, sports were not really my thing, but I made the best of it each time. I believed that was what young boys should have been doing at the time. All the kids made the very best of it, the good and the bad. I didn't necessarily have a favorite teacher.

Footnote: I didn't see what was ahead of me, so there was no need to be anything other than a normal kid. However, the enemy had plans to destroy me at early age.

I was also never a teacher's pet, but I did have a favorite subject during middle school. I loved mathematics! I believed that it was easy, and I loved counting. This subject has actually remained my favorite all the way through high school and college. Math always made me excited during class.

I was able to do it and willing to teach others if necessary! I knew I would be dealing with numbers no matter what career path I decided to take. I can't say that I was necessarily a leader during my middle school years, but I was definitely not a follower. I was never the type of kid who followed every kind of trend, posse, or gang. I was my own person, and I made my own decisions.

I had one best friend who lived next door, and he was pretty much the only person that I hung out with at one period of time during middle school. I was not attracted to joining large groups or crowds created within the school.

Footnote: Bad company has the power to corrupt good character! It also has the power to create a monster.

My next-door neighbor was my best friend up until we became 7th graders. He ordered X-rated movies on the cable box and never mentioned it to me or anyone else. My parents found out, and I was punished.

I was held accountable and had to pay for it. Our friendship ended very quickly shortly afterward. I became close to another good friend named Anzio, and we clicked instantly and always hung out. I gained another friend as well named Carlos. He was Hispanic, but color and nationality never mattered to us.

We always talked about Pokémon, Yu-Gi-Oh, and cartoon tv shows during middle school. We were very good friends until I transitioned to Ely High School, and he attended another. There were other students that I made friends during middle school like Kenneth, AJ, and a few others. We all went to different high schools afterwards. There were some students that I never saw again.

Footnote: All the enemy needs is "one" door to usher in demonic spirits. Please watch what you allow to go into your ear and eye gates.

Many others that did graduate with me from the high school that I attended. During the summer before entering middle school, I started to gain a lot of weight. I was always "easy on the eyes", but as I continued to gain weight, seemingly, my features begin to disappear. A few of my skinny cousins started to call me "chunky soup," "fat boy," and at other times, they would simply just call me "fat!" I was not comfortable being called these names, but it became normal for me.

I couldn't fight against the truth, but the truth did hurt. I will never forget a time when my father's side of the family hosted an event to show off our talents and to fellowship as a family. This family event was held in Pompano Beach, Florida, and was a perfect meet up for our family to catch up, love on each other, play games, and eat good food together. However, it took a turn for me. Some of my family members had not seen me in a while, so my weight gain caught a few people off guard.

One of my uncles looked at me and said, "hey fat boy."

Footnote: Seemingly, name calling is funny, but not when it is killing someone internally. One name can be the cause of someone taking their own life: tread lightly.

As he said this to me, my father was gathering both my uncle and I to take a picture together. I did everything that I could to hold back my tears from the pain and embarrassment I felt from his offensive way of saying hello to me. After the picture was taken, I ran to the bathroom and burst into tears. I was not comfortable being fat, and I was also not comfortable with anyone believing it was nice to call me fat either!

I was very handsome, but I started to hate how I looked. I recall riding on the school bus one day and joining in on a laugh after a funny joke was cracked on the back of the bus. I was laughing very hard, much harder than anyone else, and immediately the joke was on me. One of the girls, an upperclassman, begins to crack a joke on me. She was sort of the "lead" of the clique on the bus, so whatever she said was definitely going to draw attention to me.

Footnote: Abuse is not always physical, and it is not always intentional, however, it can happen, and you may not be aware of it. Name calling for any child can cause them to battle with an identity crisis.

She said I looked like the monkey off of the movie Aladdin, so for three years during middle school, I was called Abu by others on the bus. Because of this, I transitioned into high school with a complex trying to portray to be a bit tough, but I was also scared. I had to brace myself for what was to come, but I had other things on my mind other than the high school curriculum. I was exposed to nudity and pornography again when my best friend ordered the x-rated movies at our house. This triggered me to want to know more and feel more.

I secretly stayed up late nights watching HBO erotic movies. Eventually, I became caught up into hardcore porn through other hidden VHS tapes in our house and DVDs that were created by some of my uncles and cousins. Pornography started to cause me to lust after women as if they were nothing but a thrill.

Footnote: When a child is uncomfortable in their own skin and is also mocked and made fun of by others, this can also open a door for the enemy to make him/her feel worthless. This battle usually starts in the mind; their perception of themselves becomes tainted.

Although I had never had sex with them physically, I did it mentally. As time went on, I started to masturbate so much that I needed medical assistance and a prescription.

Footnote: Masturbation can start out enjoyable, but it can also lead to spiritual and mental destruction.

Jeremiah 1:5 (NIV)

"Before I formed you in the womb, I knew you, before you were born, I set you apart; I appointed you as a prophet to the nations."

Chapter Two

"High School"

During my 7th grade year of middle school, there was this older black man with white hair that came by our house and prayed for my family. He anointed me as well and pronounced that I'd be a preacher. I renounced the desire for such a thing. I couldn't even fathom this at all with all the things that I was battling on the inside. I was not only mingling with pornography; I was experiencing an identity crisis.

While I was in the 8th grade preparing to transition to high school, I remember looking into the mirror and then at my 5th-grade picture, and I was in total disgust. I continued to reflect on my "skinny days," and honestly, I hated what I had become. I didn't like looking at my present pictures because they reminded me of how much I had fallen from my previous self. In all sincerity, as I began to grow up, girls took more notice to me. However, I never really noticed it!

I wasn't flattered by the attention at all. I battled in this area terribly. Before I knew it, I was transitioning to high school.

Footnote: Identity crisis has no age discrimination!

This was very exciting; I must admit, but I had no idea what to expect, but I knew it was an entry into my full experience as a teenager. Although I was interested in what high school would offer me, I was still very much in a relationship with myself and pornography.

My exposure to it years before high school caused me to pursue it in full force. I discovered that HBO would show erotic movies at night, and I desired to know what sex really felt like. I started to experiment, and to me, it was very sensational. I loved it! This was not healthy for a kid my age, but I had no idea of the danger and very demonic stronghold that it would have on my life.

However, as I transitioned into the 9th grade, my family and I attended a state church function in Fort. Pierce FL. I was very afraid of the next chapter of my life, so I gave my life to Christ during this small youth meeting in a hotel where the event was held. Everything in me knew that it was time to give God my life for real.

Footnote: An addiction usually starts as a simple thought, and then a simple act.

This is where my journey, the battle in my mind and spirit truly began. It was a journey I had not prepared for.

During my first year in high school, I continued to compare my past with my present, and it was really depressing. At night, I began to pray that God would kill me because He made me repulsive. I was starting to hate myself. I would cry, asking God to kill me because I hated the image of me that He had created. In all reality, I hated the image of God.

One night I wrote a letter to my parents saying I wish I was dead, and that God would take me out of this world because I was ugly. That same night my parents were in shock to know that I even felt this way. They consoled me by telling me that there were individuals that were envious of me and my appearance, that I was handsome and had pretty great qualities. Ironically, I didn't believe them because of the negative perception that I had of myself was fixed.

Footnote: *The lack of self-love often becomes the lack of love for God as well.*

My auntie Janice took me out to eat at a restaurant once while I was going through this dilemma, and she even told me that I was very handsome.

I still did not believe that I was attractive. The perception of one's self is paramount to reality. Besides this lack of value within my own mind, I was also battling with this complex as a raging porn addict that would later open doors for demonic influences. I remember being at a picnic during these trying times, instead of sitting with everyone else, I secluded myself from everyone to another location at the park and began to cry. I still hated my reflection in the mirror!

My father saw me and came over to talk, but I was not receptive. I'll never forget the awful words that I spoke to him that day, "I wish I were never alive, and I wish you were never my dad." That statement ripped through him like a knife through his chest. All my dad could say was, "Wow!" He got up from the table and walked away.

Footnote: When someone hates who they see when they look in the mirror, they may also develop a lack of love or appreciation for those who are around them.

He no longer wanted to be a part of the picnic because his heart was broken. About ten minutes, later I called him back over to apologize. I told him that I was extremely sorry for what I said to him, and that I really didn't mean it. My father was relieved to hear my apology, but I could tell that he was still hurt. Our relationship was restored over time, but I regretted saying those words to him every day.

My perception of my personal image started to get better over the years, but this was only the beginning of my bondage. Every night, I made it my prerogative to stay up to midnight around to watch these erotic shows and movies so that I could have a sexual experience. The decision that I made to masturbate turned into a habit, and soon after, this habit became an addiction. As I transitioned into high school, I couldn't go to sleep until I masturbated. I can't remember a night or day that I did not masturbate.

Footnote: One addiction usually leads to another, and sometimes the next addiction is "self!"

I had become addicted to pornography, and I was also addicted to masturbation. When LimeWire was first created, I downloaded porn on CDs and played them on my PlayStation 2 console. I would lock myself in my room, trying to be oblivious to my parents. I did not want them to know what their innocent son was doing behind closed doors. My addiction had become so bad until I started masturbating multiple times per day, every opportunity that I had.

I was headed down a very long, hard road. Sadly, my addiction was beginning to hurt me physically. My male organ began to hurt terribly, but still, I wanted the feeling of an orgasm no matter what I suffered physically. My flesh would be pulling me, and so would the pain. I would choose my flesh and deal with the consequences of the pain later.

However, the pain became unbearable at some point. Eventually, my parents had to have me examined. I received a prescription to assist me with the pain, but that didn't stop me.

Footnote: Addictions have the power to destroy you physically and mentally.

I felt like a drug addict for porn. This addiction began to control my thoughts and my life.

I started buying porn from stores and stealing it from some of my relatives just to watch on DVD at home. I would sneak around when my parents left home for work and indulge in my sinful pleasures. I went to school fantasizing and thinking about pornographic ideas on women; an urge of sexual explosion wanted to erupt from my perverted corpse, but I only released it at night before bed. My thoughts became my worst enemy. I couldn't wait to get home and be alone.

During my first year in high school, I remember a very well-known, honorable, and respected Pastor counseled me concerning my sexual issues. Later on, I met others that would forever impact my life. At one point during this time of my life, I attended an abstinence retreat.

Footnote: *This is not a normal life for a teenager at all.*

The Pastor of this church, Arthur Hall, Church of God in Christ, at this time, assigned his prayer team and staff to host this retreat in hopes of encouraging youth and young adults to live a life that was holy and acceptable in the sight of God. They shared with us the importance of living this kind of lifestyle and different ways that we can obtain it.

Afterward, they had a ceremony where we made public vows to God that we would remain sexually pure, undefiled, and free of promiscuity. Once we made our vows unto God, we all received rings that would be symbolic to the vow and public declaration that we made to ourselves, and a reminder to keep ourselves only for marriage. I made this vow! I wanted to be pure, and I wanted to be pleasing in God's eyes. I desired strongly to be free from my addiction.

After I made those vows, sadly, I only kept them externally and temporarily. The moaning and groaning of my flesh became greater than my desire to please God.

Footnote: It is not enough to just want change; you must also fight hard for it!

The desire for ejaculation was more appealing than spiritual, sacred consecration. I was trapped by my own desires, constantly committing habitual infidelity against the Creator for a 30-second fix that never satisfied me. I made a vow with my mouth, but my heart wasn't fully committed.

I had a ring to show for it, but not the ability to value the symbol. Like many of us, we make a vow to God, we have all the symbols of religiosity and we mean well, but our cravings for sin are more luring than the Savior Himself. Whenever my flesh would want it, I satisfied. I would sin, ask God for forgiveness. I sin some more and ask Him for more forgiveness, and then sin even more and ask for His forgiveness again.

Reluctantly, I sat on my bed one night and asked God to take this enslavement away. I had finally realized that I was in love with my enemy. I was infatuated with the poison that was killing me.

Footnote: *Deliverance will always be hindered if you are in love with what you hate.*

Honestly, I came to the conclusion that I only asked God's forgiveness not so I could be sincerely changed, but so I wouldn't go to hell. I really only wanted insurance to escape hell, but no newness of life.

I loved my sins, and they loved me. Any love that I had for God was pretentious and superficial. My true Lord, lover, and master was my own flesh. I was drowning in my own fleshy desires, and the truth is, God was not as important as I really desired Him to be. God was on my mind, but He was not on my agenda!

In the 9th grade at Blanche Ely High School, I began contemplating what type of career I wanted to pursue; architect, football, and so many avenues interested me. However, every thought that I had concerning a future career was always linked to glorifying God to some extent. I wanted to do something for God in my career. Whatever I decided to do, it was going to have something to do with building the kingdom of God. I wanted to please Him!

Footnote: There is nothing more frustrating than desiring to do God's will but is still forced to try to live a normal life.

I heard about a revival at a church, Thomas Temple COGIC, where my grandfather, Robert Lee Robinson, was the Pastor. I inquired about the details of what a revival was, and I attended expecting to seek for something great. My grandfather brought in an inspiring two-week Christmas revivalist, Evangelist Roosevelt Cox. As he expounded the word of God, something hit me like a flash of light illuminating my conscience. I saw that man of God preaching from the pulpit, preaching the unadulterated, uncompromising Word of God.

That was the moment that I knew! Within myself, I said, "I know what I want to really do with my life." I couldn't explain it, but I knew! The revival was completely life changing. I started having this incredible urge for the word of God; all I could see myself doing for years is preaching the gospel.

Footnote: No matter where you are in your life, when you are called, God will continue to pull on you in whatever way that he desires.

One night I came home after speaking with my cousin, who was an Elder of this church, the Late Jeffrey Lovett Sr. about becoming a minister. As I sat in my room, there was this overwhelming desire to preach that came over me, and I began to cry profusely. I went into my parent's room in this same manner. All I could say was, "I want to be a preacher, I want to be a preacher, I want to be a preacher." They were dumbfounded and told me to wait on my timing.

Having this knowledge was surely a burden, a weight, and a blessing that would haunt me for years, even now. Throughout my years of high school, I began to turn my back on God because of my addiction to my sinful habits; pornography and masturbation. I started acting like other kids, trying to fit in, but deep down in my heart, I still had this overwhelming desire to please God and become who He had created me to be. I was literally stuck in the middle of should I do right or remain comfortable doing wrong. I was progressively losing who I was in the midst of it all.

Footnote: The weight of the call is far greater than the fall!

I did not play sports during high school, but I did join the marching band in the tenth grade. I remember the moment that I had joined the marching band at Ely High School, under the leadership of Mr. Richard Beckford. I chose to play the trumpet, the same instrument that my father played during his high school years. I was very interested in learning to play the trumpet and was ready to experience what my father somewhat experienced while he was in his high school band. It was a great opportunity for me.

Although I joined the band, I was still battling my addiction and my internal battle of who I was and what I desired to be. Not to mention my spiritual life was a wreck! My behavior took a tremendous turn for the worse. I didn't know if I would become better or worse. I was easily offended, and my respect for my parents began to decrease.

My cousin Jasmine played the trumpet as well. She was very good, but I would consider myself average at that time.

Footnote: Addictions and sin can destroy your entire life!

I was actually jealous of her playing ability; she received more recognition in the section than I did. I remember my mother dropping her off one night after band practice, and she said to me to make sure that I practiced when I got home. I was highly offended!

When my mother and I reached home, she agreed with Jasmine in reference to me practicing. I started to act up immediately! My dad was home and heard the situation starting to escalate. I was very disrespectful to my mother. My father insisted that I head into the garage so that he could talk to me about what was going on, but as soon as I walked into the garage, I grabbed a utensil to harm him.

I have no idea what came over me because I would have never considered hurting neither of my parents. My dad noticed it and said to me directly, "Son, I don't want to have to beat my son's ass. I'm not going to let you harm to me; I will protect myself."

Footnote: Sin causes most people to be easily offended. This is an indirect act of internal anguish.

I eventually put the weapon down, and the situation defused. My father and I went back into the living room to talk again, but I became furious, and we started to argue again.

I got up to walk out of the house, but as I grabbed the doorknob, the forte of my father's voice echoed once again in my soul, "If you walk out of that door, I'll beat your ass." Did I believe my father would really beat me? I'm not sure, but I knew that he cared about me. That scare tactic was definitely effective because, above all, I knew he was sincere about his threat towards me. The situation defused again.

My parents sought counsel for me; my complex became just a little better. I played the trumpet all the way through my senior year during high school. I actually became the section leader during my senior year. I enjoyed being a part of it, and I believe we were an amazing group of students. Our band made a superior rating in a marching band contest, symphonic band contest, and jazz band contest.

Footnote: The lack of self-control is one piece of evidence that you are disconnected from God.

We also went to New Orleans for a Marching Band Contest. Unfortunately, we experienced a huge amount of hate and racism in New Orleans. This was the main reason why we didn't win this particular competition. I was upset but thank God for our and director, who always knew how to keep us levelheaded and hoping for better. I wasn't considered as popular during high school, but I did become a sort of a lady's man during my senior year.

It was cool, but honestly, it wasn't my thing. Consequently, I did flirt and mess around with some of the girls on campus, but I never went the extra step because I vowed to remain abstinent. I was doing well as band member, but my struggles and internal battles did get worse. I tried to suppress it in many ways with my irreverence for God, but it was still present. The weight and shadow of it was always upon and near me.

Footnote: Purpose will always sneak up to remind you of who you really are.

During my last six months as a senior, I dedicated myself to attending Florida Agricultural & Mechanical University in the Fall of 2007 with a partial band scholarship. I believed this would be the right direction for me at the time. As the summer had commenced, my cousin Scooter (*Vondrell*) came to live with us. We attended Sunday school together, and I felt my desire beginning to grow again for the word of God more. The more I got involved with Sunday school, my understanding of the word of God started to shift as well.

My ability to expound on the WORD of God was very present. At times I would even shock myself. I was so passionate about teaching the word of God. My cousin and others who attended were able to identify it, but I continued to suppress it. The desire to preach became more stronger than ever before.

Footnote: When God calls you, he will also qualify you.

Jeremiah 29:11-12 (NIV)

For I know the plans I have for you," declares the LORD, "plans to prosper you and not to harm you, plans to give you hope and a future. Then you will call on me and come and pray to me, and I will listen to you.

Chapter Three

"College"

Preparing for college was a very reluctant and exciting time for me. I was interested in going to a secular college, but my desire to study theology began to increase, so I experienced many mixed emotions during the process. However, that was easier said than done! Seemingly, everyone wanted me to go to FAMU, but I wanted to pursue something that was in direct correlation to my calling. I wanted what was connected to God.

So, I attended FAMU, but my heart wasn't in it. I became a member of the infamous Marching 100 rattlers. However, in the second semester, I sought purpose by changing majors like psychology to religion. The second semester of school was trying for me because I wanted my true purpose; I wanted to preach! I started to become very angry with both of my parents for "sending" me to this college because they knew what my heart truly desired, but they did not offer me any guidance, clarity, nor direction.

Footnote: It's okay to take advice, but always follow your heart's desire.

I knew I had a calling on my life; therefore, I began to seek God for answers.

I would walk the campus of Florida A&M University, and I always envisioned myself preaching. I felt as if God wanted more from me; to step out of my boat. I met some well-rounded individuals in Tallahassee as well as good friends that'll never be forgotten, but it was time to make a decision to pursue my calling or to settle for a secular degree. After much prayer and frustration, I decided to make preparations to leave Tallahassee and to find another path would lead to my God-given purpose.

I chose not to speak with my father right away about it because he wasn't walking in his own purpose. He wouldn't understand. I knew my dad wouldn't agree with my decision. I was afraid, but I felt like obeying God was more important than facing my father. I desired to follow God!

Footnote: Listening to everyone else will cause you to ignore God!

Besides my father, I felt like everyone else also wanted me to do what they wanted me to do instead of what God had called me to do. This brought on so much stress upon my mental faculties, and it brought fear and trepidation in my heart. I knew that no one in my family would understand the severity and weight of such a call from God. However, as I traveled back home, I continued to pray to God for an answer. Simultaneously, my dad wanted an answer as well as others about my next move.

I felt completely lost and confused because I was both sincere and scared, yet no one seemed to be compassionate, reasonable, or even tried to understand. I contemplated leaving the country to go to Africa or Jerusalem to seek God for an answer after returning home. I felt like I would never receive a direct answer from being in the company of those around me. I needed seclusion and isolation before the Lord. Above all, I needed peace of mind and to be able to clearly hear the voice of God.

Footnote: The lack of purpose causes the lack of direction.

During church service on a Sunday morning at Thomas Temple COGIC, shaking and nervous. I announced that I would be leaving the country for a while to head to Jerusalem. This moment turned into complete chaos! My mother ran up to grab me, and I immediately began to weep. People started to circle all around me, attempting to counsel what they clearly could not understand.

After that particular event, a few other encounters occurred with my father about what happened during service. In his opinion, he believed that I was running away from my responsibilities of being a man and growing up, but I wasn't. I was actually willing to do the one thing that he had failed at doing his entire life; listening to and follow the call of God on his life. My father ran from the call of God on his life while I ran rigorously towards mine. Two extremes headed in opposite directions.

With no real solution, I decided to take on a job at a local LA Fitness Center.

Footnote: Purpose is a sacrifice that many people won't understand; go after it anyway!

During the summer, I was hired as one of their janitors. I was always a great worker, but eventually, the enemy came after me. At that time, I was pursuing a genuine relationship with a young lady, but she was not interested. That kind of rubbed me the wrong way, I started to feel like my soul was being pierced with negativity; things just weren't going right.

One day, as I walked up to go into work, as usual, a black hummer pulled up on me, a window rolled down, and a stocky, overweight Spanish guy started to speak to me. He had two kids in the car with him, but he continued to say, "you have a lot of negativity in your life." He made some other predictions as well concerning the young lady that I was interested in, and that he can help me with the situation. I was very desperate for answers, so I got into the vehicle with him. He passed me one of his business cards and asked me to meet him at his office.

Footnote: Desperation can be very dangerous or even deadly!

I decided to meet with him that night. Once again, I got into his car again and tested him, but he only repeated himself. I asked him to tell me my middle name, and he countered with, "Though shall not test the Lord thy God." I agreed with him because it seemed as though he really wanted to help me. I wasn't getting it from anyone else, so this seemed like a last resort.

I went back to his office later that week, and he gave me a pebble to rub, hold, and meditate with. He told me to write down my name numerous times on paper and to "sow" into him for getting rid of the negativity that was in my life. He also gave me a small capsule to soak in for twenty minutes when I got home. He even told me to increase the monetary gift for the "Father, Son, and the Holy Ghost." Although he seemed to be helping me, for some reason, he always wanted me to keep these things a secret and to tell no one.

Footnote: The enemy comes to steal, kill, and destroy; there's nothing good about him!

Then, his wife got involved. She told me that they were going to do a ceremony on me so that they could get rid of all the negativity around me. She instructed me to go to BrandsMart and target to purchase instant credit cards to give to them, which I did. I took $500.00 out of my bank account and gave it to them. I was completely unaware of what I was getting myself into.

One night, while I was in my room, my father came to me saying that he noticed that I withdrew money from the joint account we shared. He thought it was for school, but I reluctantly told him about the situation, and my life quickly began to crumble. I became really afraid. People started coming to the house and praying. Consequently, I found out that witchcraft, had been performed on me which really scared me even more.

I started feeling angry inside and mad at God because I felt betrayed and unanswered. Honestly, I began to hate God.

How did I get myself caught up in this kind of evil?

Footnote: God is always listening to our prayer, yet he will only answer in his timing; wait on Him!

Witchcraft is the use of magic by the conjuring of spells, enchantments, or items to manipulate people's minds or situations. It is the process of trying to get what you want anyway that you can, or hurting someone who you do not like, are jealous of, or just simply want to see dead.

This is a very wicked and evil act! It is practiced amongst many cultures and groups of people who believe strongly in it. Witchcraft is not done by human beings alone, yet it is also done through the assistance of demonic spirits. Before transitioning into college, I had never heard about witchcraft, and I never knew what it really was in detail. While attending college, I still did not know anything about it.

It was never my desire to discover any specifics about it, and honestly, I was probably too young to even care too much about it. I was dealing with my addiction, desiring more of God, and trying to work on becoming a better person.

Footnote: Be very careful of who you turn to for help!

I actually found out about witchcraft after I dropped out of college. I came into the knowledge of this wicked activity through this situation. My life started to spin completely out of control!

Matthew 11:28-29 (NIV)

"Come to me, all you who are weary and burdened, and I will give you rest. Take my yoke upon you and learn from me, for I am gentle and humble in heart, and you will find rest for your souls.

Chapter Four

"Mental Illness"

My young adult experience did not start so well. I never thought that I would battle with the things that I had faced and were still facing in my life. If someone had told me that I would battle with pornography and masturbation addiction, become rebellious and disrespectful towards my parents, drop out of college, or that I would interact with Vodou, I would have never believed it. I desired to be the man that God had created me to be, however, the path that I was on seemed to be leading me in the opposite direction. I was losing control in ever are of my life, including my mind.

In August of 2008, I decided to enroll in the Atlantic Technical Center for an automotive mechanic trade. I attended class and learning the profession, but still, something in me just didn't sit right. This was not my calling, and it was not my purpose here on earth. I was still feeling very angry internally; I felt like a beast in a cage or the incredible hulk at times.

Footnote: When you feel like you are losing control, you probably are! Turn to God quickly!

There was so much rage on the inside of me, and I was unaware of how detrimental this was to me mentally.

One day before attending class, a very dangerous thought came to mind to purchase a razor blade and cut my arms. I did not defeat this thought; instead, I stopped by the store and decided I was not going to school anymore. At this point in my life, I was very angry at God. I felt like he had failed me, but I wanted to take it out on myself. I was very hesitant at first about cutting myself because I had never done anything this extreme, but I went for it!

I took the razor and lightly swiped it across my forearm; instant blood started to flow. As I drove towards my mother's job, I continued to slice my arms. Soon, they were dripping badly with blood. I began to curse God with many indignant words, many curse words; "You piece of sh%$, MotherF&%@, Son of a bit$@." When I arrived at my mother's job, I walked inside and shocked all of the employees, including my mother.

Footnote: The enemy has a way of causing you to harm yourself; flee from him!

As my mother approached me, I began to ask her, "Why won't God answer me? Why won't he give me an answer? Why won't he talk to me? I'm going to keep slicing until He answers!" I cursed the name of God so much that my tongue grew numb.

They called the Boca Raton police dept. I went to attack one of the officers and was immediately tased for the first time in my life. I was restrained and put into an ambulance. My mom was standing there in total shock, with tears running down her face. All she could do is wonder what had happened to her son.

They took me to the hospital to bandage my wound and strapped me to the bed so I wouldn't hurt myself any further. I was later relocated to an outpatient mental hospital, where I was also admitted. I just laid there, reflecting on how I ended up in this situation. One thing that I knew for sure was that I was extremely angry with God. I felt as though He had betrayed, left, and hated me.

Footnote: God will never leave you, but if you leave Him, you may feel like he has left you as well.

I became so much more enraged with God that I wanted to kill Him; wishing that I was the one that could kill Him over again at the cross of Calvary. I remember my mom sending me my bible; I threw it in the trash as an incentive to God that I didn't care anymore. There were times when I would curse God to see if He would take action and kill me. I didn't have a passion for living anymore, and I blamed Him. I believed strongly that everything that I was going through was all of his fault.

During the winter of 2008, things sort of cooled down. I was on a lot of prescription medication, which caused me to gain an additional 30-50lbs making me around between 250-270lbs. I wasn't too happy about the meds nor the added weight, but seemingly this was all helping me become normal again. Unfortunately, as I was about to start school again, I began to become very anxious. I started to cut myself again; all I thought about was homicide and suicide.

Footnote: Be very careful with how you allow your anger to dictate your behavior towards God. Things could get worse for you!

This time I was admitted into Imperial Pointe Mental Hospital on the 6th floor. Upon my first admission into this hospital, I was very quiet, but then I began to scream out in outrage that I wanted to kill people. This caused me to be put inside of an all-white room. They gave me a shot of medicine and strapped me to the bed. I was forced to remain isolated away from the other patients and staff.

I went in and out of the mental institution for about three years. During these times, I would hear voices that would tell me to run in front of a moving train or jump out of the car on Interstate 95. I made strives to do so, but my mother would always say, "if you keep testing God, He'll take His hand off of you!" I went through this vicious mental cycle continuously. I had thoughts of killing people in my mind, going on a killing spree, and even thought about going to my church to shoot everyone, including myself.

I remember being in Imperial Point Hospital listening to music in my headphones, and all I could do was cry.

Footnote: A mind is terrible thing to lose, especially to the enemy.

All I thought about was committing a homicide. When I would be permitted to go home, the medication that I was taking made me sleep all day. Not to mention, I was still gaining more weight from my constant eating. I would still hurt myself from time to time, I still watched pornography, and I would listen to hardcore rap and gospel music.

I would feel hopeful at times about life, but then there was this one particular time when I felt like all hope was gone. I decided that I would try to take my own life. While I was at home, I grabbed all of my prescription medication and swallowed them. I laid down on the sofa, and I started to feel like I smoked marijuana, but then I started becoming disoriented.

I jumped into the shower to try and wear it off, but to no effect. I began to fall all over the shower and started calling out to my sister for help. She called 911, and they came quickly! As laid, there thinking that I was going to die, I told God, "I don't want to die." I swallowed the pills, but I really wanted to live.

Footnote: Suicide is NEVER the answer!

I passed out once more and woke up in the hospital the next day. I gave everyone that I knew quite a scare! They sent me back to Imperial Pointe once again, but this time I remained there for almost a month. I was suffering from mental illness. Mentally, I was not healthy at all.

My mind was not working efficiently and appropriately to fulfill its designated task. I did not have the ability to think appropriately. My mind was not whole; it was sick. Mental illness is characterized by disturbances in thought (as delusions), perception (as hallucinations), and behavior (as disorganized speech or catatonic behavior), by a loss of emotional responsiveness, and extreme apathy. It is a noticeable deterioration in the level of functioning in everyday life.

This is also considered as a mental disorder or disruption of the normal or regular functions of the mind. It is the opposite of harmony; it is chaotic and causes much confusion mentally.

Footnote: Mental illness is REAL; do not pretend that it is not real!

A mental disorder, also known as mental illness, affects every aspect of a person's life: hygiene, socially, mentally, relationally, etc. Consequently, mental illness is really a paralysis of one's thoughts; a person mind can't cope with life, a disruption of the thoughts, and a mind that is out of its original alignment. I experienced all of this firsthand.

There were times I'd sit in my room for hours and regret that I ever dropped out of college at Florida Agricultural & Mechanical University. I regretted not enjoying or experiencing the "college life" as I should have. I would resent family members and friends because they were having these experiences and I wasn't. I felt insecure and constantly compared my current life at that moment to my cousins, who were still in college. I always assumed that if I had never dropped out of school, I would have never been exposed to the witch, warlock, and the mess that I was in.

Footnote: Don't' drown in your regrets and past mistakes. God is the RESTART button.

I questioned myself daily about the what ifs. I wanted to press a restart button and redo everything that I had done prior to experiencing all of this. This was not the life that I wanted for myself, and the enemy wanted me to believe that this was the life that God gave to me. This caused me to be angrier, and my father knew it. I wanted to change the decisions that I had made so that I could undo the present, but the damage was already done.

I just wanted another chance to redo my life and fix what was wrong. I felt so forsaken by God because He would not deliver me! One day I actually got up at my church and said "F%@$ God, and F%@$ Jesus," ran out in desperation for God to kill me. I also decided that I wanted to be homeless; but my family did not allow it to happen. This affected my entire family, especially my parents.

It was a complete shock to my family; they never experienced anything like this ever in their lives.

Footnote: The enemy loves to make you feel alone; reject his lies!

I was embarrassed sometimes, and other times I just felt alone because no one understood what was happening to me. No one could help me that desired to so desperately. I was in this very scary world all by myself, but I was also surrounded by so much love and support. I am still so very grateful.

I recall many times trying to move forward; I would register for classes a Broward College in Coconut Creek, Atlantic Technical School, or other endeavors, but whenever I would take the steps to go, I would become extremely anxious and fearful. I remember signing up for an accounting class as well. I started to do the work, and I literally began to have an anxiety attack because doing something new and beneficial was scary to me, and I was very unsure of myself. My father saw this consistent habit of me starting and stopping things, and always offered me help. This was a ploy of the enemy tormenting and bothering my mind never to move forward, and to hinder me from making any improvements in my life.

Footnote: If the enemy can have your mind, he will try to take your entire life.

I never embraced my diagnosis because I never considered it as one. I knew what I was experiencing was more spiritual than mental, and I just wanted to be delivered from it. I was very angry, bitter, regretful, and fearful; these things kept my mind racing out of control. In spite of my anger, I still wanted to be delivered. I wanted to be helped!

I actually went to a therapist, but session after session, it was to no avail. The prescriptions weren't helping me, and the Psychiatrist were over-medicating me. Due to this over medicating my body went into a catatonic state. The catatonic state is a behavioral syndrome marked by an inability to move normally. It can be associated with schizophrenia and other mental illnesses.

Catatonia may involve symptoms such as staying still, fast or strange movements, lack of speech, and other unusual behavior. Due to the abundance of prescriptions, my body started to slow down my movement.

Footnote: The enemy never shows up to play fair, he wanted me dead!

My mother had to start clothing and feeding me. These were things she started to notice. I was admitted into another mental hospital, and the next morning, I could not move my body.

I could only move my eyes and mouth. If I did move my body, it was extremely painful and hard. Honestly, some of the employees at this hospital weren't compassionate to the pain that I was feeling. On several occasions, I felt like they were ignoring me. Consequently, the hospital saw this as a critical condition, and had me admitted back into Imperial Point Hospital in Fort Lauderdale.

When I got there, my body completely shut down, and I became unconscious. On the next day, I woke up in the ICU. When my mother arrived, she said my eyes were rolled into the back of my head. While I was in this state, a friend of the family, a prayer warrior, came by to visit me. She advised my mother to sue the doctors and the hospitals because this my condition was a sign of me being brain dead.

Footnote: Your condition is not your conclusion!

My mother says her spirit didn't agree with this advice. She says the Holy Spirit whispered softly, "if you agree, so shall it be." Mother decided to believe God, and by the next day, I was awake, stable, and released from the ICU. God moved on my behalf sooner than anyone expected. Whose report will you believe?

My mother believed and trusted in God more than she did the doctors and the words of other Christians. One day my mother and I decided that we would trust God completely! We decided to put all of our faith in Him to deliver me. After making this decision, I remember concluding my life and realizing how sinful, wretched, and hypocritical that I had been towards God. I evaluated my fruit and realized that I never had any good fruit.

Matthew 7:16-18

"By their fruit you will recognize them. Do people pick grapes from thornbushes, or figs from thistles? 17 Likewise, every good tree bears good fruit, but a bad tree bears bad fruit. 18 A good tree cannot bear bad fruit, and a bad tree cannot bear good fruit."

Footnote: *You will always know a tree by its fruit.*

Matthew 12:34-35

You brood of vipers, how can you who are evil say anything good? For the mouth speaks what the heart is full of. A good man brings good things out of the good stored up in him, and an evil man brings evil things out of the evil stored up in him.

I had reached a place in my life where I knew if I had died, I was going straight to hell. I started telling God that I wanted to be holy, and that I desired to produce good fruit. I wanted to reflect goodness and righteousness. I want to be more like God and less of myself. I also wanted to have good fruit.

As a result, I purchased a book called, "The Fruit of The Spirit: Becoming The Person God Wants You to Be" by Thomas E. Trask & Wayde I. Goodall. I decided to make this investment to feed my spirit. I also began to pray more. I was becoming more serious about my relationship with God. Within this time frame, God showed me a dream of my spiritual condition.

Footnote: If you draw near to Him, He will draw near to you!

DREAM: The door to my room was pitch black, yet the door was opened. I went into the room, and the door shut. All I saw was darkness and felt nothing but pure evil. In the dream, I said, "Where is God?" ... I asked another question in the dream, "Am I not the light of the world?" .... the door opened back up, and I walked out to the kitchen.

God revealed that I was not truly in Him, and He wasn't in me. The apostle John solidifies this in *1 John 1:5-6, "This is the message we have heard from him and declare to you: God is light; in him there is no darkness at all. If we claim to have fellowship with him and yet walk in the darkness, we lie and do not live out the truth."* There was no light in the room because God was not present in me or my life. It was a reflection of a life without Him, even though I had a calling and purpose.

It was a life separated from Him.
How could I be the light of the world if He didn't reside in me?

Footnote: Self-reflection is always necessary to see where you really are in God.

How could I assist the lost if I was still lost myself? How would they find God if he was not in me? I had no genuine fellowship, communion, nor genuine relationship at the time; it was superficial.

John 12:46 says, "I have come as a light into the world, that whoever believes in Me should not abide in darkness." John 8:12 says, Then Jesus spoke to them again, saying, "I am the light of the world. He who follows Me shall not walk in darkness but have the light of life."

I decided to pursue my healing, and it happened through my deliverance. During one of our church old school revivals, I rededicated my life to Christ. Demons were cast out, and the Holy Spirit came within. God received me as his son again, and I was so full of humility. He saved me again!

Throughout the three years that I experienced mental torment, instability, and mental breakdowns, I cursed God! I did this in hopes of Him attempt killing me.

Footnote: It is so amazing how God's love never changes towards us no matter what.

Many times, I asked my mom why God wouldn't kill me for the things that I was doing. There were nights that I would lay in the bed or on the floor and cry, but I would feel the manifested presence of God come over me right after I cursed Him. I didn't understand why God would shade me after I continuously betrayed Him and slapped Him in the face with the treachery.

In this particular season of testing, I started to sing and write songs as well. I noticed that I had other gifts within me, but the gift to preach the gospel was still buried deep in my soul. No matter how much I cursed Him and hurt Him, deep down inside, I really wanted God. I was anointed to preach the gospel and to set the captive free, but I was so very bound myself. Although I was losing myself, my kingdom's purpose still had a heartbeat.

If you are experiencing mental illness right now in your life, I recommend highly that you search yourself, and ask God to help you sincerely. Be genuine about your confession before Him and the desire for his help.

Footnote: Seek after God with your whole heart for deliverance.

God knows when we are real, and when we are looking for a temporary fix. Be sincere in wanting to be healed, not just forgiveness. Acknowledge the things that you have done against God and others.

Seek out the appropriate help that will assist you mentally and spiritually. My experience being in the mental institution caused me realized that most of the individuals were there because of some high level of stress, and they "snapped," or just out of desperation did something irrational. I would also like to encourage you to manage your stress levels. Find a productive way to free your mind of worries, anxieties, and the things of this world because it can become a noose. A mind is indeed a terrible thing to lose when you have access to live a life more abundantly.

Footnote: Your physical and mental well-being is very important; take care of yourself.

John 8:36 (NIV)

"So if the Son sets you free, you will be free indeed."

Chapter Five

"Mental Freedom"

There are so many amazing things that can happen in a person's life when they experience real freedom. Unfortunately, many people miss the opportunity to live a liberated life because of their fear of leaving or being delivered from bondage. Especially those who do not have support or has no spiritual guidance. I thank God all the time for having a praying family, and for parents who wanted to help me, so they refused to abandon me. I was extremely blessed, and I am forever grateful for my life, another chance to live a fruitful, happy, productive life in Christ.

Freedom allows you to have the ability to be unhinged, uncaged, liberated, without restraints, and free from any capacity of enslavement. To me, it simply means to be able to live without being held against your will. It is an individual's right to act, speak, or think as they want without hindrance or restraint. It is the state of not being imprisoned or bound to anything that you don't want to be bound to. Freedom is the power to be your own person without permission.

Footnote: Freedom is a CHOICE!

There was time in my life when I was not free at all. I was bound to my addictions and the evil that played over and over in my mind. Not only did I have to do a self-evaluation and take inventory of myself, I also had to repent to experience my freedom. It was my responsibility to review my actions, behaviors, decisions, and my mindset to effectively evaluate where I was in my life. Once I was able to do this, I was also responsible for confessing my sins to the Lord and submitting to a changed heart.

I had become very repentive. I came to the conclusion that what I had been doing was wrong, evil, and a complete offense to God. I was ready to turn from my sin and live for God entirely. Repenting before God means changing your direction from everything else and turning to God. It is the change of your opinion or perspective that caused you to have a change in your behavior or actions towards God and sin.

For three consecutive years, many preachers came and facilitated church revivals, but there was one in, particular, that was very different.

Footnote: Repentance must be embraced to experience real deliverance.

Why? Because I was tired of being the person that I was, and I wanted real change. My uncle, Pastor Alan Robinson, hosted a revival one year. When he was done preaching one night, he asked everyone who needed something from God to make their way down to the altar. The Holy Spirit was very high in the building!

As I walked towards the alter, I immediately fell to the floor. Demons started to manifest and scream. I began to purge. Throughout the week's revival, my uncle told me that God was not through with me yet. He continued to speak and told that my deliverance was not completed just yet.

I found myself being knocked down to the floor again because of the power of God that rested in the atmosphere. Another minister came to encourage me, Elder Arthur Williams. He told me to get up from the floor and thank God for delivering me. I honestly did not think that I was delivered. I was afraid that nothing had really happened, that I would remain in torment, and I also feared the demons returning back to me.

Footnote: There is nothing like a real altar experience!

But then I heard a still small voice despite of all the loud music and shouting that said, "They won't be coming back, I'm here now." I knew it was God talking to me, assuring me that I was free and that my body had become the temple for His Spirit. After this experience, people would claim that they could see a light emanating from me, others couldn't even recognize me because I wasn't the same person that they knew before I had that experience during the revival. I was saved, born again, and knew it. I felt it, and I continued to experience the presence of God in a way I never knew.

God began to really talk to me more clearly. The thoughts of suicide and homicide were no longer invading my mind. The addictive urge to watch pornography was eradicated. I was finally living and breathing in fresh air Freedom is such a beautiful experience. Especially from demonic spirits and evil thoughts.

Footnote: If you really want to be free indeed, surrender.

Freedom has allowed me to become more stable mentally, emotionally, in my behavior, and my actions. I still have my up and down days, but the Holy Spirit always leads and guides me on how to embrace and handle them. The keyword to continual growth and change is progress! I was afraid to move forward or do different things, but now the limits and chains are gone, and I'm not afraid to move forward. Freedom has actually taught me how to appreciate the trials and tribulations that I have gone through.

I look back every now and then and realize that God used those experiences to humble me and to cause me to look solely to Him for help. Freedom has also taught me that God has the power to set anyone free from any form of bondage; porn, depressions, drugs, sex, lies, self- mutilation, etc. He is a miracle worker!
I experienced freedom when I acknowledged that I was the problem to my problems. I stopped blaming God and took full responsibility for the things that were going wrong in my life.

Footnote: *Honesty leads to deliverance!*

I threw myself at God to heal me of my mental and spiritual plight. I was desperately chasing after Him for my deliverance. I desired to be free more than anything else I wanted in my life. If you desire to be free and live an abundant life in Christ Jesus, I encourage you to fully depend upon the grace of God to change you. It will produce life changing results in your life as it did in mine.

I was not set free because of my good works or because of my name, but because God's grace was sufficient for me. Grace saved me! *1 Corinthians 15:10 says, But by the grace of God I am what I am, and His grace toward me was not in vain; but I labored more abundantly than they all, yet not I, but the grace of God which was with me.* Grace in Greek is "Charis," which means to rejoice, in English, it means charity. The word grace is used to express when a person of dignity or status would come to the aid of someone helpless and hopeless and could not repay the favor.

Footnote: *Grace can't be purchased!*

Charis was a term that meant to show kindness to someone in need; they couldn't earn it or merit it, it was just given by the kindness and compassion of the individual. That's what grace is for; it helps the helpless, the hopeless, and those that know they can't earn it. God is kind towards the hopeless and helpless situation; he will free you base upon His charitable heart. We are saved by the grace of God, not by our own works of righteousness. Salvation, healing, and deliverance are free because Jesus Christ paid the price we couldn't afford.

"Experiencing freedom will require you to do a few things. First, believe that you can be free (Hebrews 11:6)! Faith must be activated in order to receive it. If you have any doubt, God will help your unbelief by proving His power (Mark 9:24). Next, you must acknowledge the areas that you are bound, that you have a problem, and that you really need help. James 5:16 tells us to confess our sins, errors, and false steps to one another that we may be healed.

Footnote: *Freedom has requirements, please submit to them.*

This word heal in the Greek is "iaomai," it literally means to heal, cure, and restore back to health. It was used mostly for healing physical diseases and affliction, but it also related to demonic oppression and spiritual restoration in Luke 9:42, 1 Peter 2:24-25. This word, when translated in Hebrew, is "rapha", 2 Chronicles 7:14, Isaiah 53:5). Don't keep your sins a secret; where there are secrets, there's no healing or restoration. You must be willing to expose your sins to receive the healing you desire.

Confess your sins not just to God but find someone you can confide in about your sins. While I was repenting before God, I was also confessing my hypocrisy and sins to my uncle Alan and my cousin Dianna. Most times, I would go to Dianna to share my struggles because we had a much stronger bond. There were also others that I confided in as well. If we don't confess our sins to one another, we could sabotage our own healing.

Footnote: Sometimes, it is very hard to trust people, but in order to grow and mature, you will always need to trust somebody.

Seek after professional and spiritual counseling, a licensed therapist, and Pastoral assistance to help you experience real deliverance. Lastly, in sincerity, ask God for freedom; many times, God didn't deliver me because my desire for freedom was superficial. Ask, and it will be given to you, but ask with a sincere heart, Matthew 7:7. When we do what God asks us to do, He'll fulfill His part. Then, He becomes the God who heals, Jehovah Rapha, Exodus 15:26.

Once you obtain it, keep it and cherish it. Please don't just remain stable in your freedom. Grow into the freedom that God gives you by the renewing your mind and the safeguarding of your heart. Live the life that God desires for you to live. You were not created to live in bondage; you were created to live, move, and breathe in FREEDOM!

Footnote: Be FREE!

Resources

- **Journaling Saves Lives**

"Journaling Saves Lives is a mental health advocacy organization that facilitates educational seminars for the community to eliminate the stigmas of mental illness. This organization also serves as a liaison to connect individuals and/or families who are directly and/or indirectly dealing with mental health problems to peer and professional resources to help them along the path of healing & wholeness.
JournalingSavesLives@yahoo.com
Twitter: @JournalingSLUSA
Facebook: @JournalingSavesLives
YouTube: Journaling Saves Lives

- **National Suicide Prevention Lifeline**
suicidepreventionlifeline.org
1-800-273-8255

- **Mental Health Association Of Central Florida**
www.mhacf.org
407-898-0110

- **Florida Depression Helpline**
floridadepressionhelpline
24/7 Helpline: (866) 267-5177

- **Lee Mental Health**
www.saluscareflorida.org
239-275-4242

- **Anger Management**

www.helpguide.org

- **National Alliance of Mental Illness: NAMI**

www.nami.org

1-800-950-6264

- **Assistance To Quit Porn Addiction**

www.covenanteyes.com/

- **Stress Management**

www.webmd.com

- **Crisis Text Line**

Text Hello to 741741

- **Major Depression**

www.betterhelp.com

contact@betterhelp.com

- **Mental Illness Assistance**

www.mentalhelp.net

1-877-307-4205

Author's Contact Information

Antoine D. Thurston

AntoineThurston@yahoo.com

www.AntoineDThurston.com

Facebook: Antoine Thurston

Instagram: Antoine Thurston

"Don't give up on God because He hasn't given up on you."

My Bondage & My Freedom

"From The Mental Institution To The Pulpit"

Made in the USA
Columbia, SC
17 August 2020